I0519094

"To play without Passion is inexcusable".
- Ludwig van Beethoven

HERMANN
—PRESS—

This book presents classical sheet music from the public domain,
meticulously edited by Damian Hermann to closely mirror the original compositions.

Our goal is to deliver an authentic experience and score to our readers.

Copyright © 2024 by Damian Hermann

All rights reserved.

Extended edition

ISBN 978-1-964383-04-0

Published by

www.HermannPress.com

WELCOME

To: 'ICONIC SONGS'.

This *step-by-step* guide teaches you five
Beautiful piano songs in a very practical way.

These songs progress through the eras of
Classical and romantic music and are the immortal
Proof that the feelings and thoughts of these
Brilliant composers are still alive
For all musicians today.

Consistency is key and with just a couple of minutes
A day you will get the most out of this book.

BECOME TODAY'S MASTER

Table of Contents

Instructions p.3

Circle of Fifths p.4

Prélude in C major
Johann Sebastian Bach

Original Music Score.............. p. 6

Sheet with Numbers (123)........ p. 9

Letters & Numbers (ABC/123).... p. 12

Gymnopédie no.1
Erik Satie

p. 16 ....Original Music Score

p. 19 .... (123) Sheet with Numbers

p. 22 .... (ABC/123) Letters & Numbers

Für Elise in A minor
Ludwig van Beethoven

Original Music Score.............. p. 26

Sheet with Numbers (123)........ p. 30

Letters & Numbers (ABC/123).... p. 34

Nocturne in C# Minor
Fréderic Chopin

p. 39 ....Original Music Score

p. 44 .... (123) Sheet with Numbers

p. 49 .... (ABC/123) Letters & Numbers

Marche Turque
Wolfgang Amadeus Mozart

Original Music Score.............. p. 55

Sheet with Numbers (123)........ p. 61

Letters & Numbers (ABC/123).... p. 67

INSTRUCTIONS

Each song in this book follows three steps. The first step is the original score. Next you have the version with finger numbers added for all notes. Lastly you'll get the complete score with finger numbers and note letters.

BASIC THEORY: NOTES & CLEFS

The treble clef tells you that the note around the cringle is a 'G'. The bass clef note between the dots is 'F'. The notes have the same note arrangement but the order on the clef is different.

Middle C is above the bass clef and below the treble clef; so these two clefs together cover much of the range of most voices and instruments.

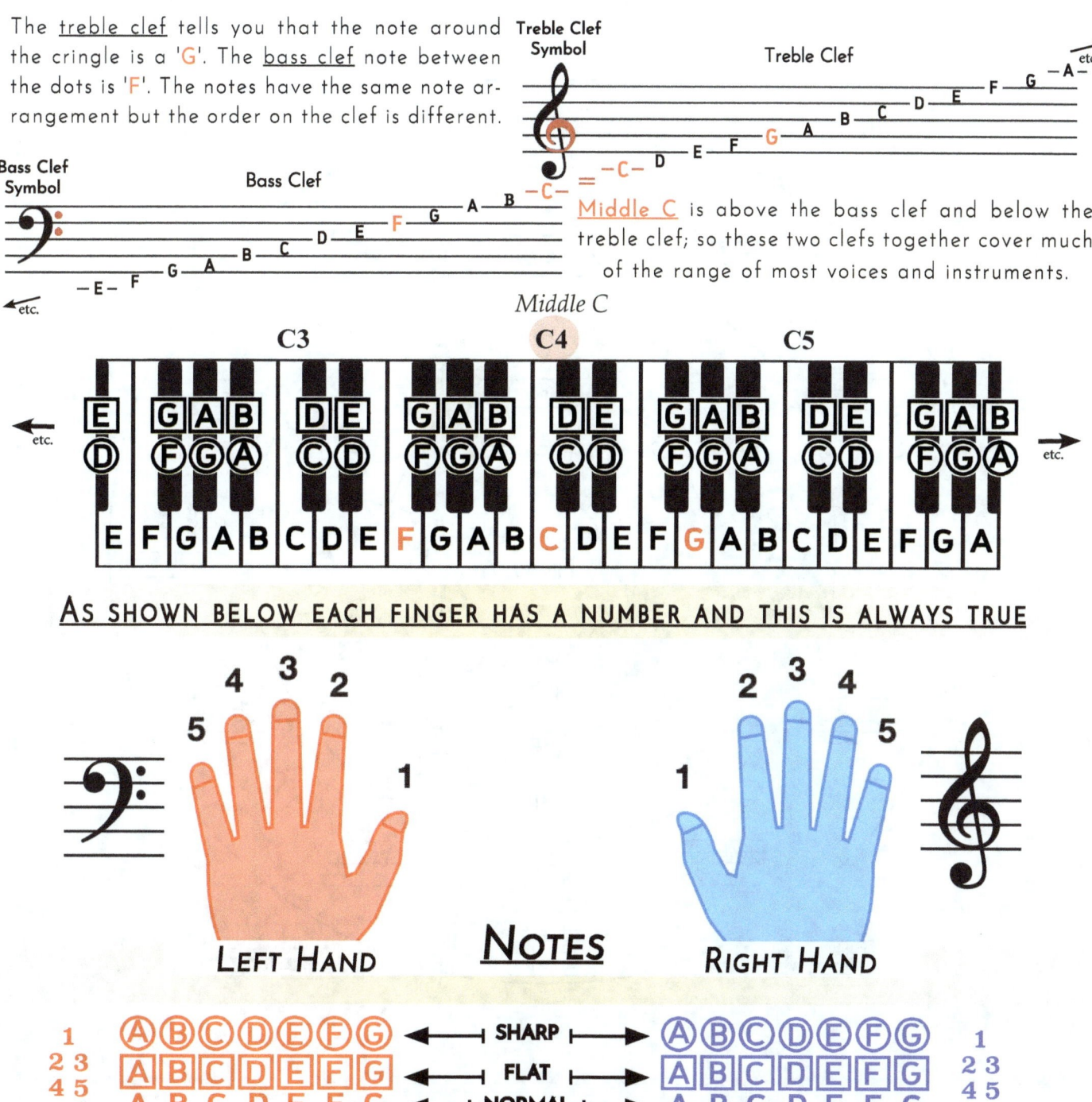

AS SHOWN BELOW EACH FINGER HAS A NUMBER AND THIS IS ALWAYS TRUE

NOTES

BLUE letters/numbers are played by the _right hand_.
RED letters/numbers are played by the _left hand_.

CIRCLE OF FIFTHS

The Circle of Fifths is a graphic representation of the relationshiphs between the 12 major and minor keys. A relative minor key exists for every major key. Natural minor scales in relative minor keys share the <u>same notes</u> as the related major scale.

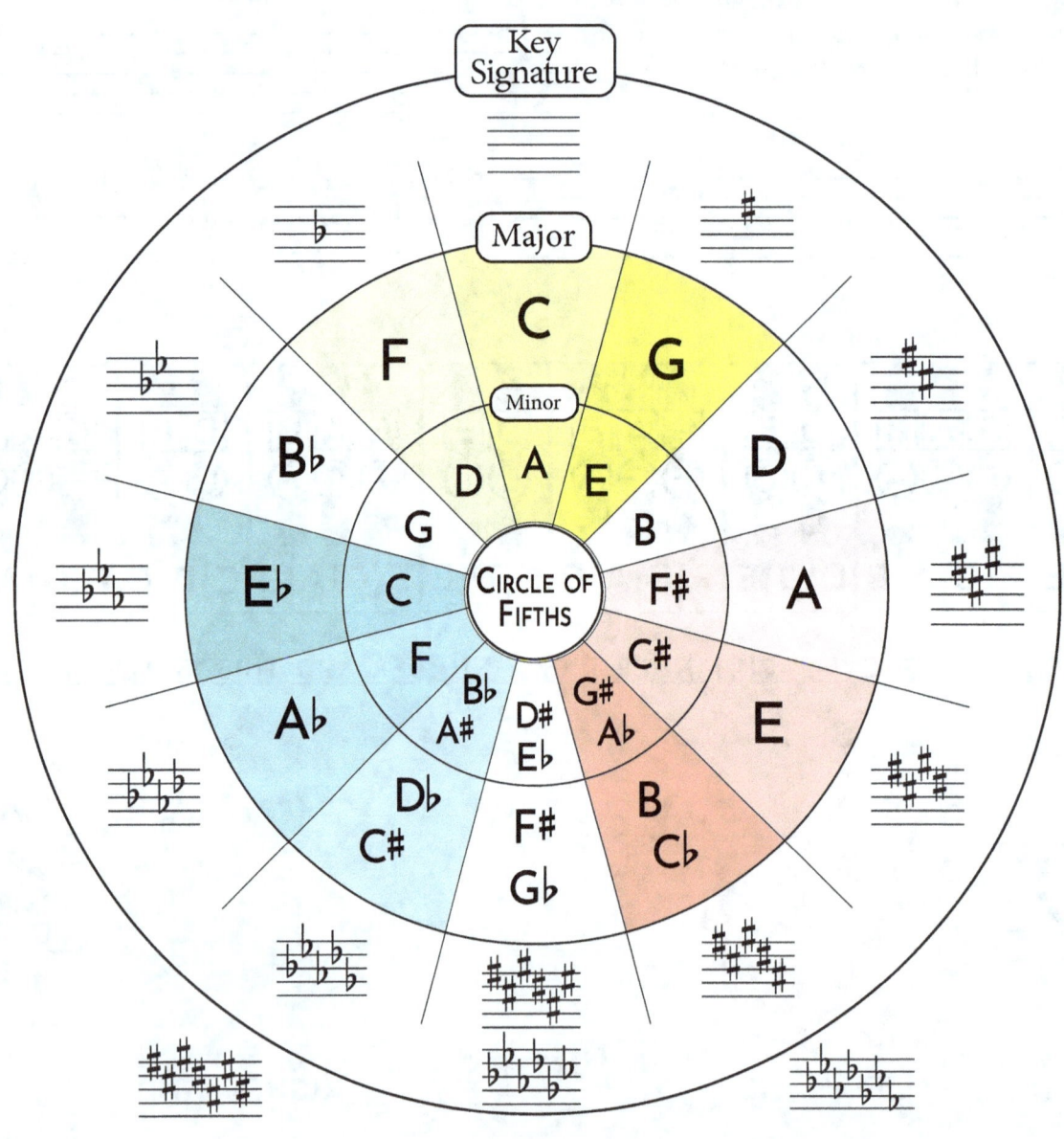

<u>ORDER OF FLATS (KEY SIGNATURE)</u>

B♭, E♭, A♭, D♭, G♭, C♭, F♭

<u>ORDER OF SHARPS (KEY SIGNATURE)</u>

F#, C#, G#, D#, A#, E#, B#

PRELUDE IN C MAJOR
from "The Well-Tempered Clavier"

Being the first song from Johann Sebastian Bach's "
The Well-Tempered Clavier," composed in 1722, this prelude has an arpeggiated, flowing melody that spans the entire keyboard.
It is a great choice for beginners due to its simple structure and consistent rhythm of notes, which help you develop finger independence and feel for the keyboard.

The following tips will help you to practice and become better.

1. START SLOW

It is very important to play each note correctly, and doing so at a low speed first helps you build the necessary muscle memory. Don't worry about keeping up with the original speed or setting a metronome.

2. FINGER NUMBERING

Pay close attention to the finger numbers, especially in the number version of your sheet music.. Remember that to play smoothly, you need to be able to place and move your hands well.

3. PAY ATTENTION TO THE RHYTHM

A metronome can be very helpful. Set the speed to a low level first, and as you get used to the beats, slowly speed it up.

4. BREAK IT DOWN

Focus on small areas at a time. Mastering a few measures at a time can help you feel more confident and make sure you play correctly.

5. SEPARATE, THEN TOGETHER

Work on each hand separately to focus on its difficulties. As soon as you feel ready, start playing with both hands.

6. READ THE NOTES

Practice reading the original score. If you are unsure, go to the third version and look up the name.
This helps you become a better musician, learn more songs in the future, and move past the beginning level.

7. SAY OR SING

Say or sing the note names out loud as you play from the version with the note names.
This will help you remember where the sounds are on the piano and the staff.

8. RECORD YOURSELF

Document your practice lessons from time to time so you see what you need to work on and how you're doing by listening back over time.

9. REGULAR PRACTICE

It's important to practice often. Also, having short daily practices is better than long ones less often. Being consistent is key and will bring you the best results.

10. THINK ABOUT FINGER TRANSITIONS

Consider how the fingers change places, especially where the finger numbers are shown. Composers also include those numbers in original scores because your performance will sound better and flow better if you use smooth changes.

Prélude No. 1 in C Major

from "Das Wohltemperierte Klavier" Book I

BWV 846

Johann Sebastian Bach

Piano

Prélude No. 1 in C Major

from "Das Wohltemperierte Klavier" Book I
BWV 846

Johann Sebastian Bach

Prélude No. 1 in C Major

from "Das Wohltemperierte Klavier" Book I

BWV 846

Johann Sebastian Bach

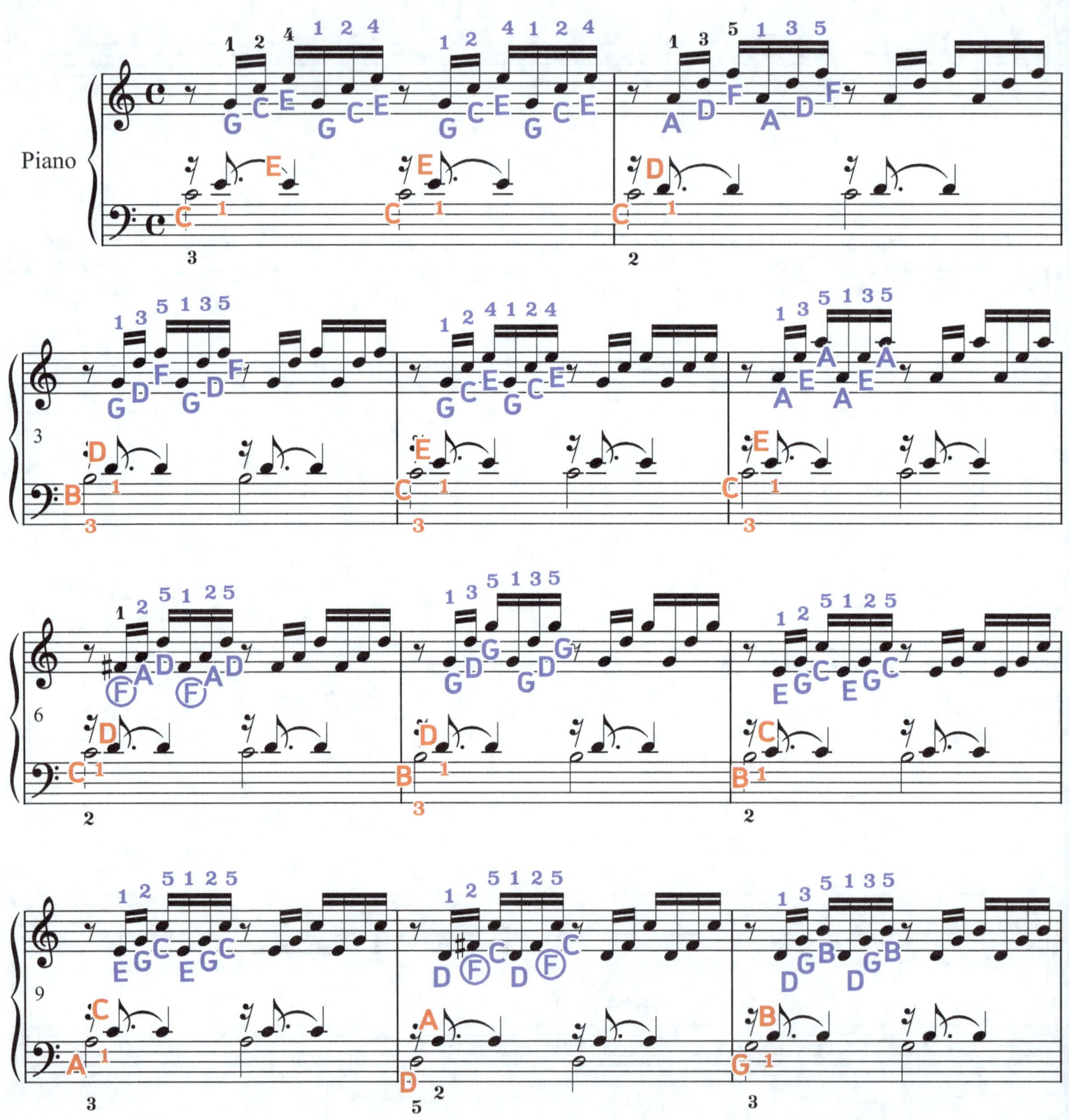

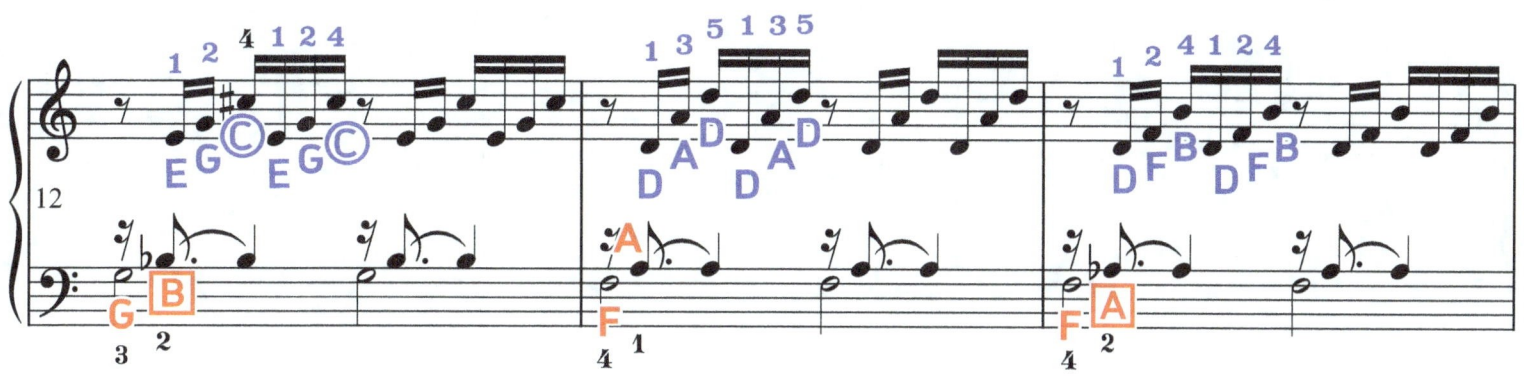

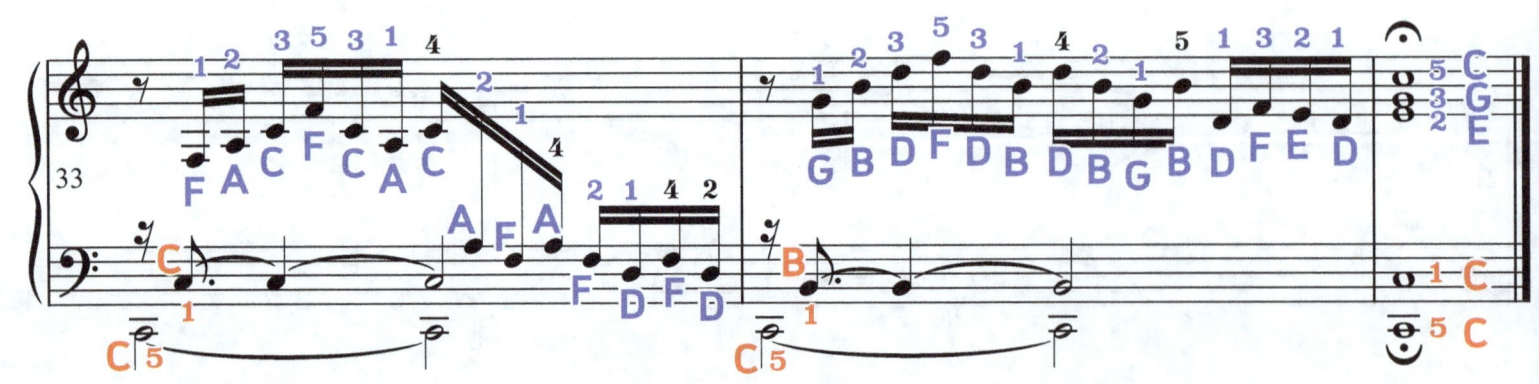

- 3 -

14

GYMNOPÉDIE NO. 1
from "Trois Gymnopédies"

Our second song choice is Erik Satie's "Gymnopédie No. 1," composed in 1888. A peaceful and sad composition that teaches you about expressive playing and tempo control making it perfect for learning how to blend emotion and technique. Its dreamlike mood is also ideal for mastering subtle dynamics and pedal use.

The following tips will help you to practice and become better.

1. START SLOW
It is very important to play each note correctly, and doing so at a low speed first helps you build the necessary muscle memory. Don't worry about keeping up with the original speed or setting a metronome.

2. FINGER NUMBERING
Pay close attention to the finger numbers, especially in the number version of your sheet music.. Remember that to play smoothly, you need to be able to place and move your hands well.

3. PAY ATTENTION TO THE RHYTHM
A metronome can be very helpful. Set the speed to a low level first, and as you get used to the beats, slowly speed it up.

4. BREAK IT DOWN
Focus on small areas at a time. Mastering a few measures at a time can help you feel more confident and make sure you play correctly.

5. SEPARATE, THEN TOGETHER
Work on each hand separately to focus on its difficulties. As soon as you feel ready, start playing with both hands.

6. READ THE NOTES
Practice reading the original score. If you are unsure, go to the third version and look up the name. This helps you become a better musician, learn more songs in the future, and move past the beginning level.

7. SAY OR SING
Say or sing the note names out loud as you play from the version with the note names. This will help you remember where the sounds are on the piano and the staff.

8. RECORD YOURSELF
Document your practice lessons from time to time so you see what you need to work on and how you're doing by listening back over time.

9. REGULAR PRACTICE
It's important to practice often. Also, having short daily practices is better than long ones less often. Being consistent is key and will bring you the best results.

10. THINK ABOUT FINGER TRANSITIONS
Consider how the fingers change places, especially where the finger numbers are shown. Composers also include those numbers in original scores because your performance will sound better and flow better if you use smooth changes.

Gymnopédie No. 1

from *Trois Gymnopédies*

Éric Alfred Leslie Satie

Erik Satie
(1866–1925)

- 3 -

18

Gymnopédie No. 1

from *Trois Gymnopédies*

Éric Alfred Leslie Satie

Erik Satie
(1866–1925)

Lent et douloureux

Piano

Gymnopédie No. 1

from *Trois Gymnopédies*

Éric Alfred Leslie Satie

Erik Satie
(1866–1925)

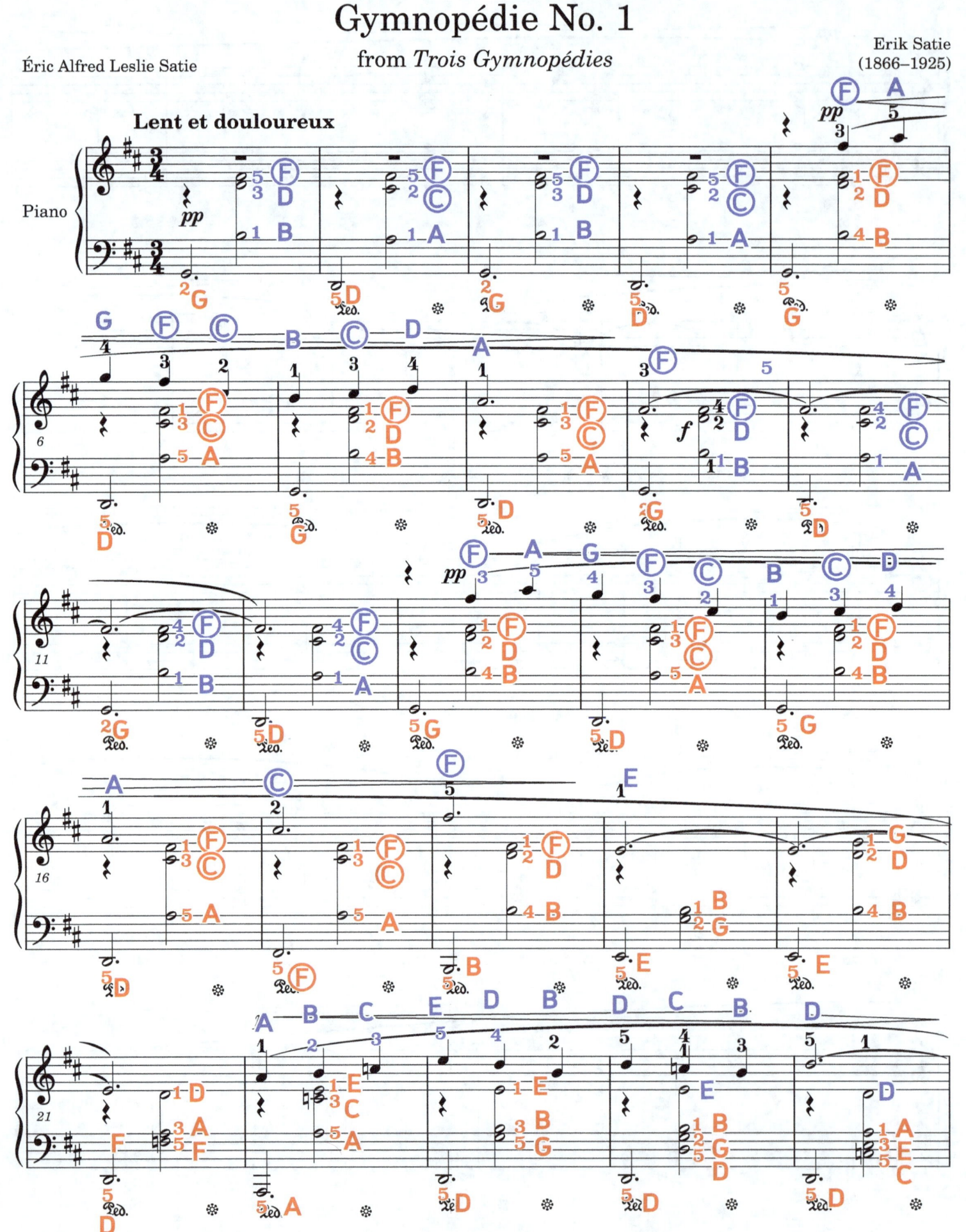

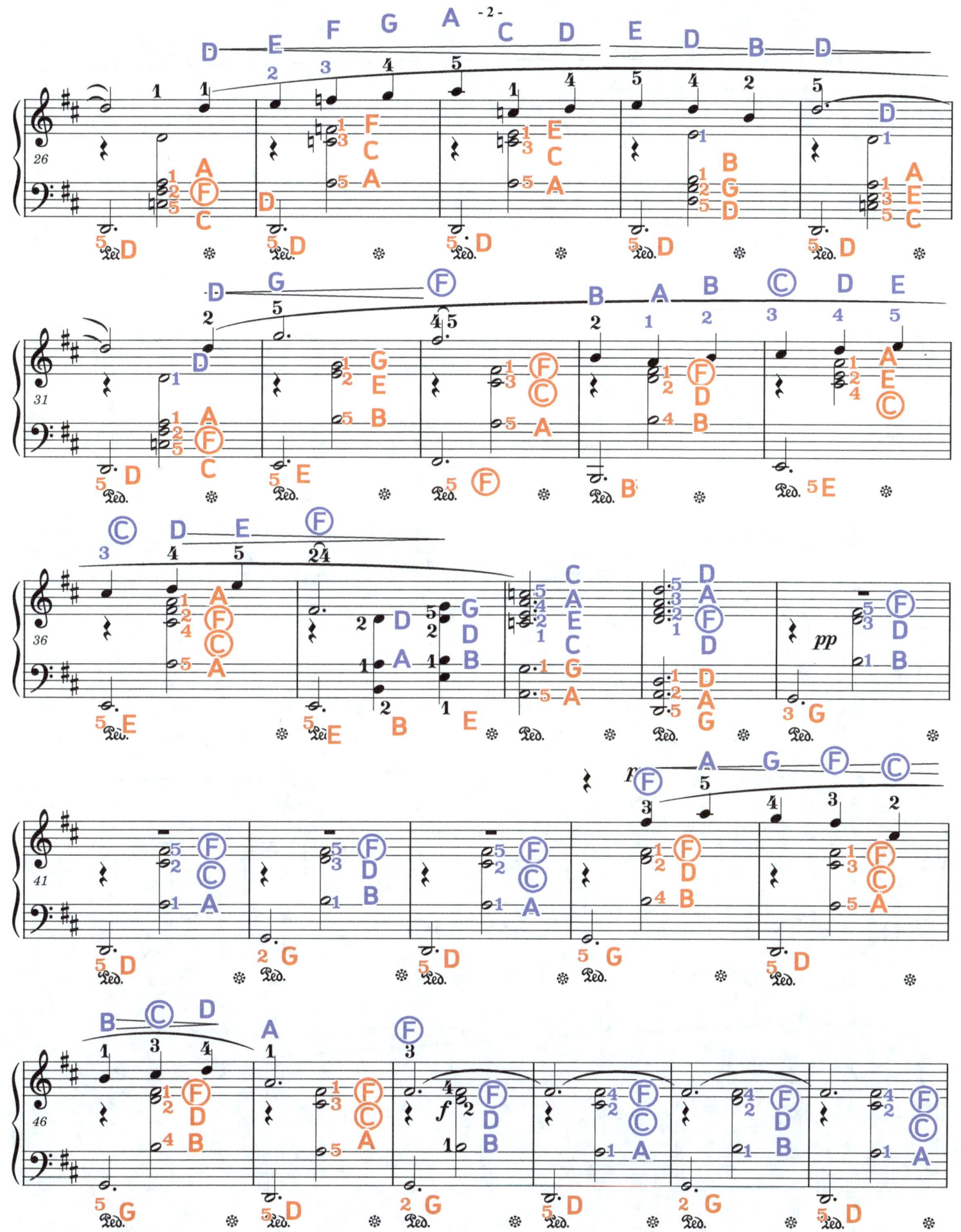

FÜR ELISE IN A MINOR
WoO 59

Ludwig van Beethoven's famous composition "Für Elise," composed in 1810, is a very popular choice among beginner pianists because of its memorable melody. It switches between a delicate theme and a contrasting middle section with lots of tension and drama. This provides you with classical music fundamentals, allowing you to explore emotional depth and technical control.

The following tips will help you to practice and become better.

1. START SLOW
It is very important to play each note correctly, and doing so at a low speed first helps you build the necessary muscle memory. Don't worry about keeping up with the original speed or setting a metronome.

2. FINGER NUMBERING
Pay close attention to the finger numbers, especially in the number version of your sheet music.. Remember that to play smoothly, you need to be able to place and move your hands well.

3. PAY ATTENTION TO THE RHYTHM
A metronome can be very helpful. Set the speed to a low level first, and as you get used to the beats, slowly speed it up.

4. BREAK IT DOWN
Focus on small areas at a time. Mastering a few measures at a time can help you feel more confident and make sure you play correctly.

5. SEPARATE, THEN TOGETHER
Work on each hand separately to focus on its difficulties. As soon as you feel ready, start playing with both hands.

6. READ THE NOTES
Practice reading the original score. If you are unsure, go to the third version and look up the name. This helps you become a better musician, learn more songs in the future, and move past the beginning level.

7. SAY OR SING
Say or sing the note names out loud as you play from the version with the note names. This will help you remember where the sounds are on the piano and the staff.

8. RECORD YOURSELF
Document your practice lessons from time to time so you see what you need to work on and how you're doing by listening back over time.

9. REGULAR PRACTICE
It's important to practice often. Also, having short daily practices is better than long ones less often. Being consistent is key and will bring you the best results.

10. THINK ABOUT FINGER TRANSITIONS
Consider how the fingers change places, especially where the finger numbers are shown. Composers also include those numbers in original scores because your performance will sound better and flow better if you use smooth changes.

Für Elise in A Minor

WoO 59

Ludwig van Beethoven
(1770–1827)

Poco moto

Für Elise in A Minor

WoO 59

Ludwig van Beethoven
(1770–1827)

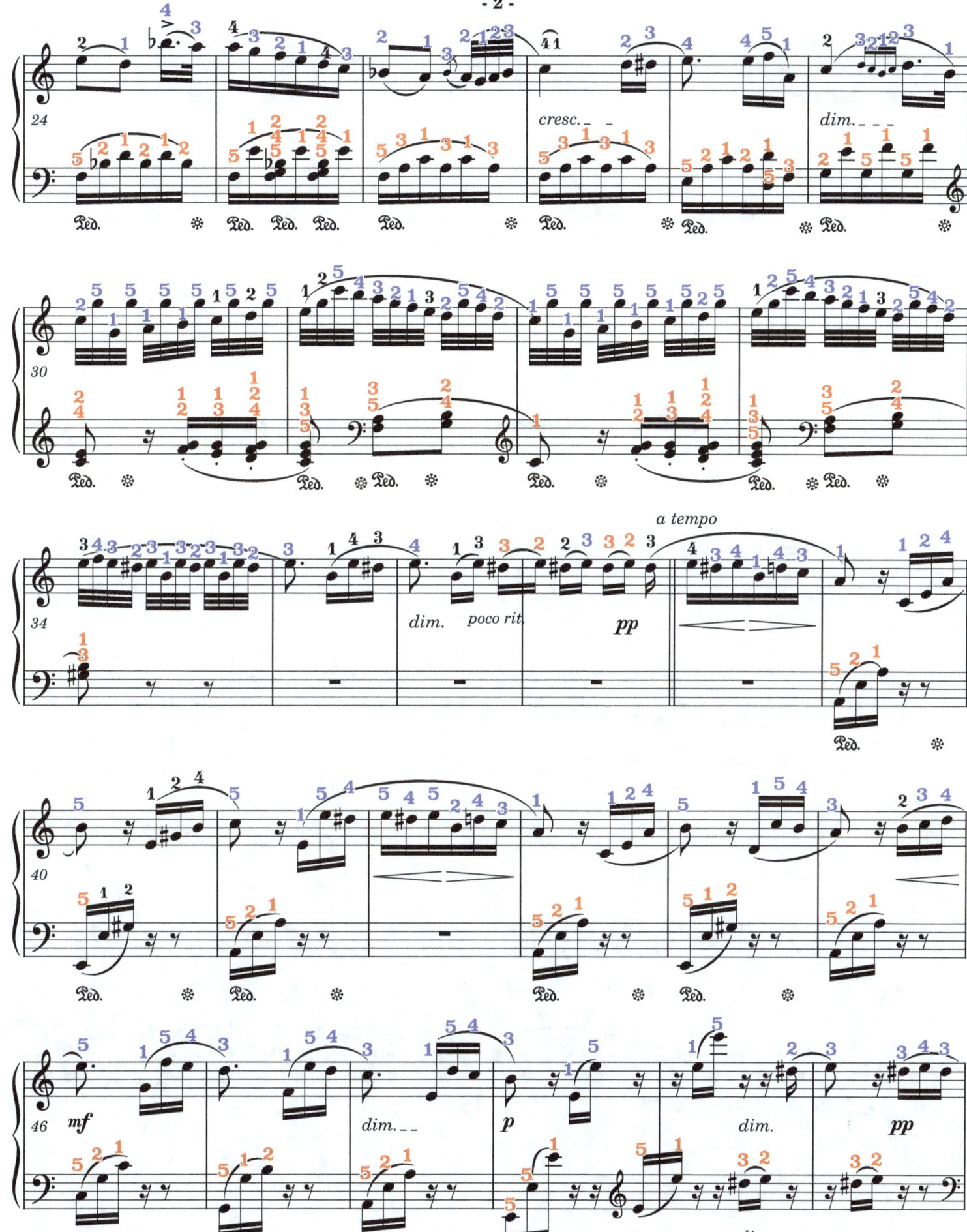

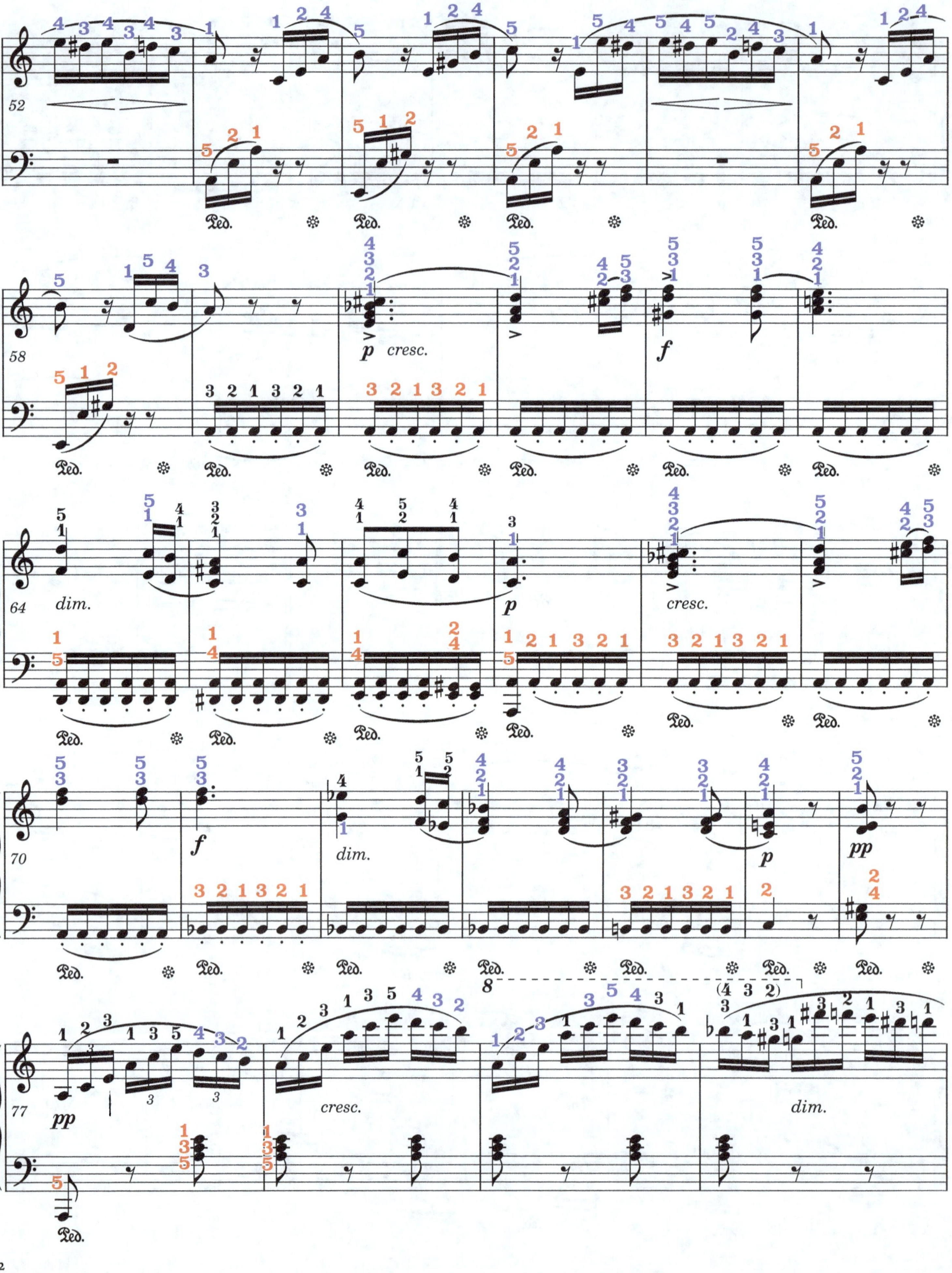
52
Ped.
58
p cresc.
f
64
dim.
p
cresc.
70
f
dim.
p
pp
77
pp
cresc.
8
dim.

Für Elise in A Minor

WoO 59

Ludwig van Beethoven
(1770–1827)

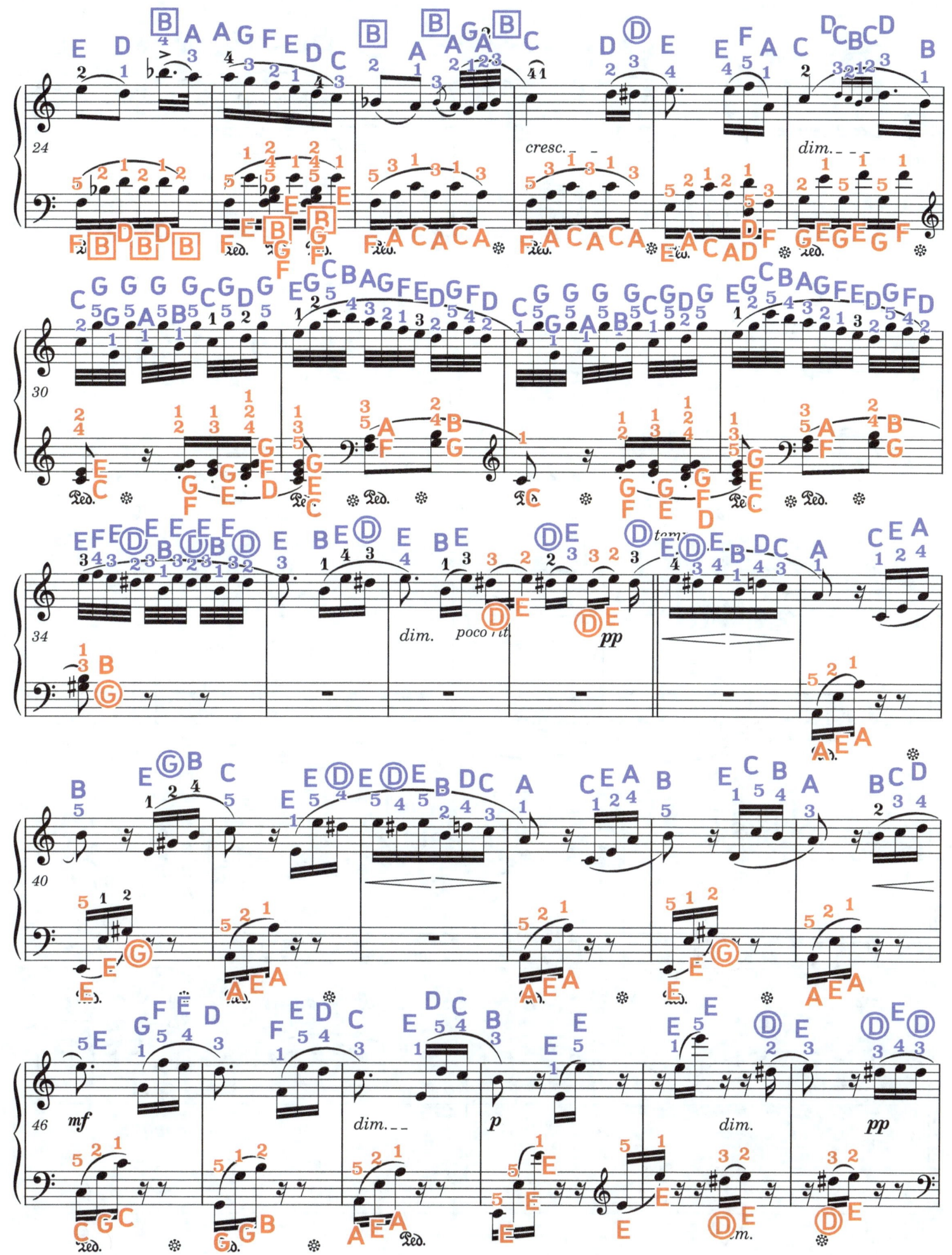

NOCTURNE NO. 20

in C sharp minor / Op.Posth

Frédéric Chopin's Nocturne in C-sharp minor, No. 20, is a more challenging song. This piece was published posthumously in 1870 and is well-known for its lyrical beauty and emotional abundance, which is typical of Chopin's compositions and grace.
Representing romantic piano music, allow yourself time for the practice of sustaining smooth legato lines and more complex musical expressions.

The following tips will help you to practice and become better.

1. START SLOW

It is very important to play each note correctly, and doing so at a low speed first helps you build the necessary muscle memory. Don't worry about keeping up with the original speed or setting a metronome.

2. FINGER NUMBERING

Pay close attention to the finger numbers, especially in the number version of your sheet music.. Remember that to play smoothly, you need to be able to place and move your hands well.

3. PAY ATTENTION TO THE RHYTHM

A metronome can be very helpful. Set the speed to a low level first, and as you get used to the beats, slowly speed it up.

4. BREAK IT DOWN

Focus on small areas at a time. Mastering a few measures at a time can help you feel more confident and make sure you play correctly.

5. SEPARATE, THEN TOGETHER

Work on each hand separately to focus on its difficulties. As soon as you feel ready, start playing with both hands.

6. READ THE NOTES

Practice reading the original score. If you are unsure, go to the third version and look up the name.
This helps you become a better musician, learn more songs in the future, and move past the beginning level.

7. SAY OR SING

Say or sing the note names out loud as you play from the version with the note names.
This will help you remember where the sounds are on the piano and the staff.

8. RECORD YOURSELF

Document your practice lessons from time to time so you see what you need to work on and how you're doing by listening back over time.

9. REGULAR PRACTICE

It's important to practice often. Also, having short daily practices is better than long ones less often. Being consistent is key and will bring you the best results.

10. THINK ABOUT FINGER TRANSITIONS

Consider how the fingers change places, especially where the finger numbers are shown. Composers also include those numbers in original scores because your performance will sound better and flow better if you use smooth changes.

Nocturne No.20

in C sharp minor / Op.Posth

Frédéric Chopin

Lento con gran espressione

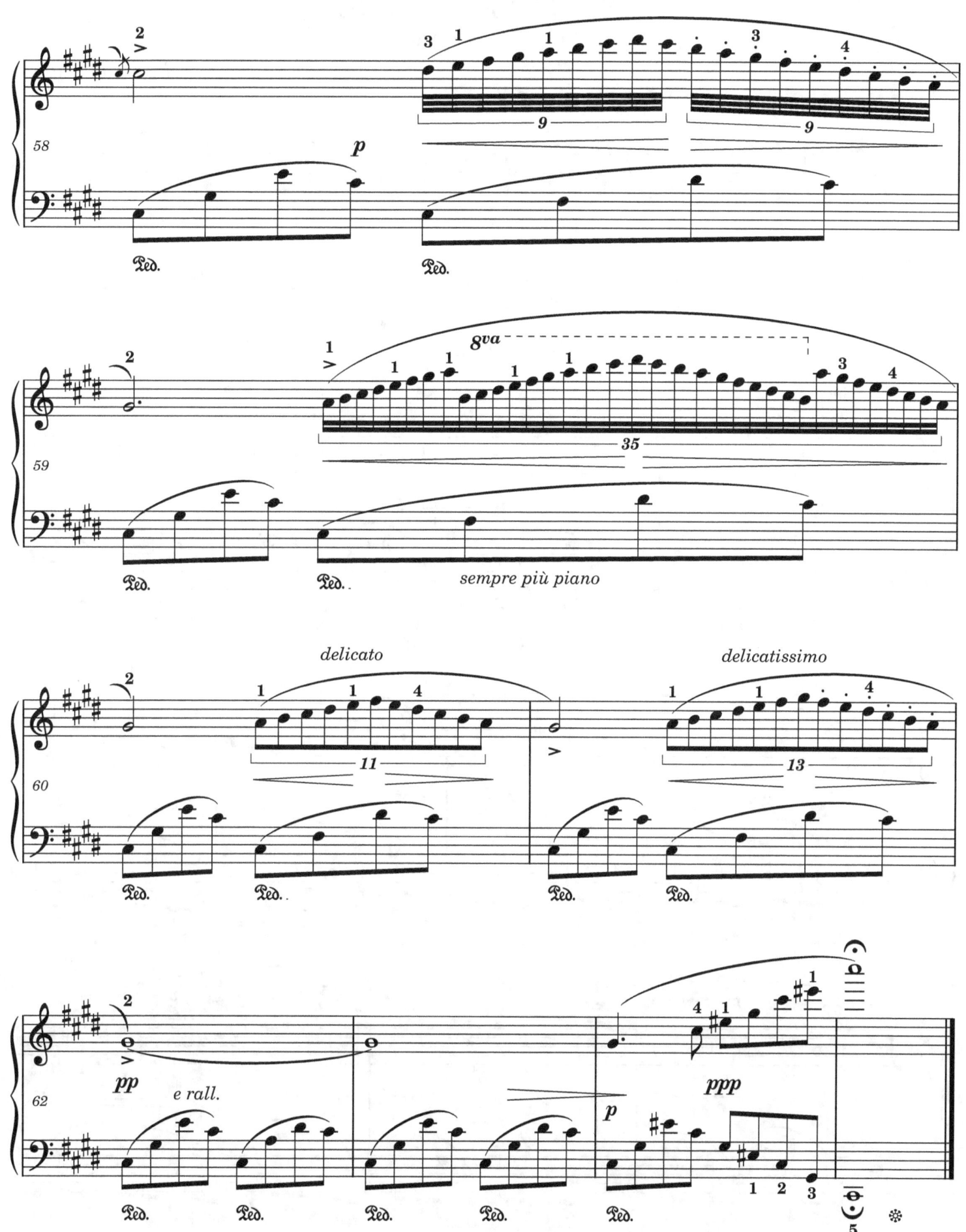

Nocturne No.20

in C sharp minor / Op.Posth

Frédéric Chopin

Nocturne No 20

C sharp minor / Op.Posth

Frédéric Chopin

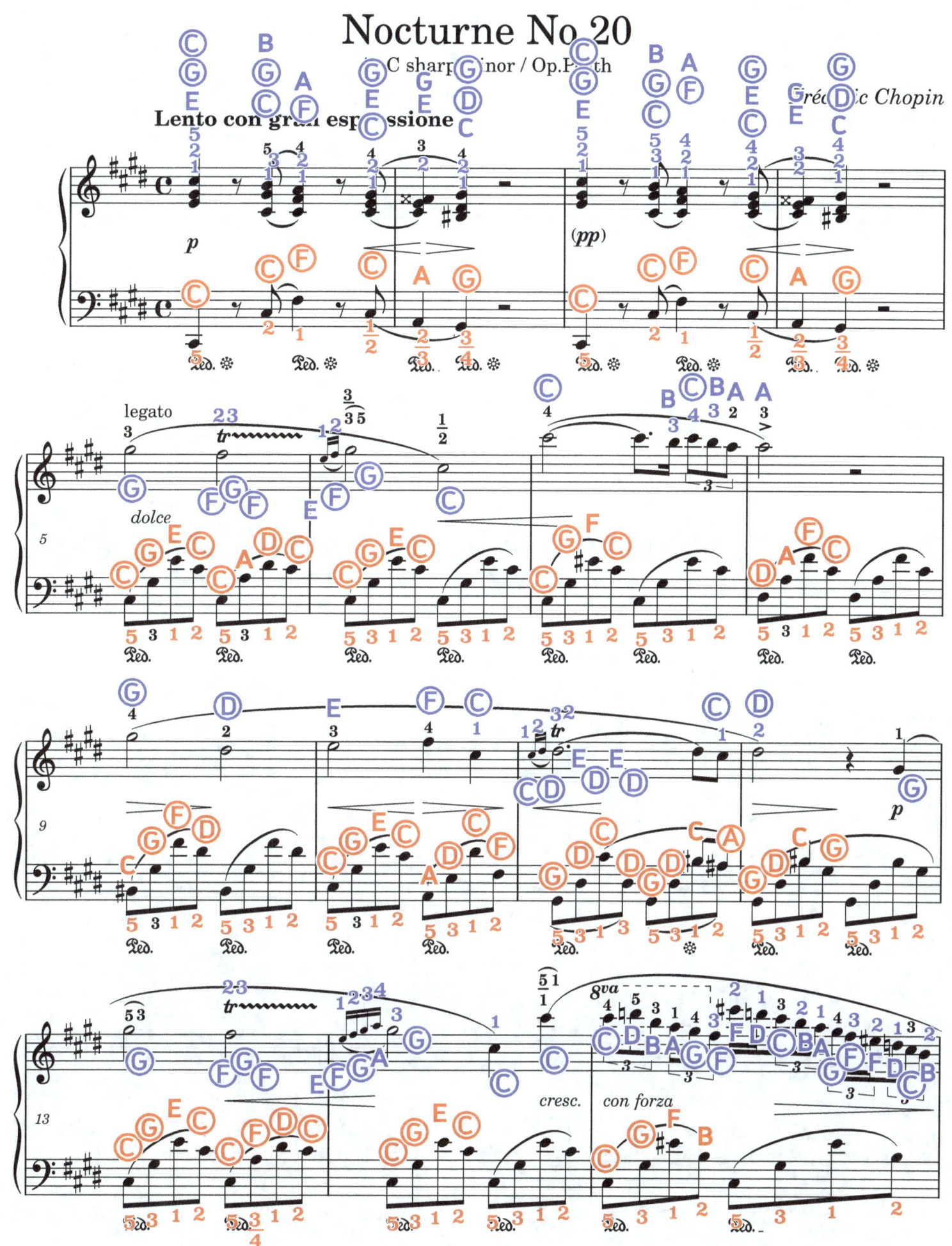

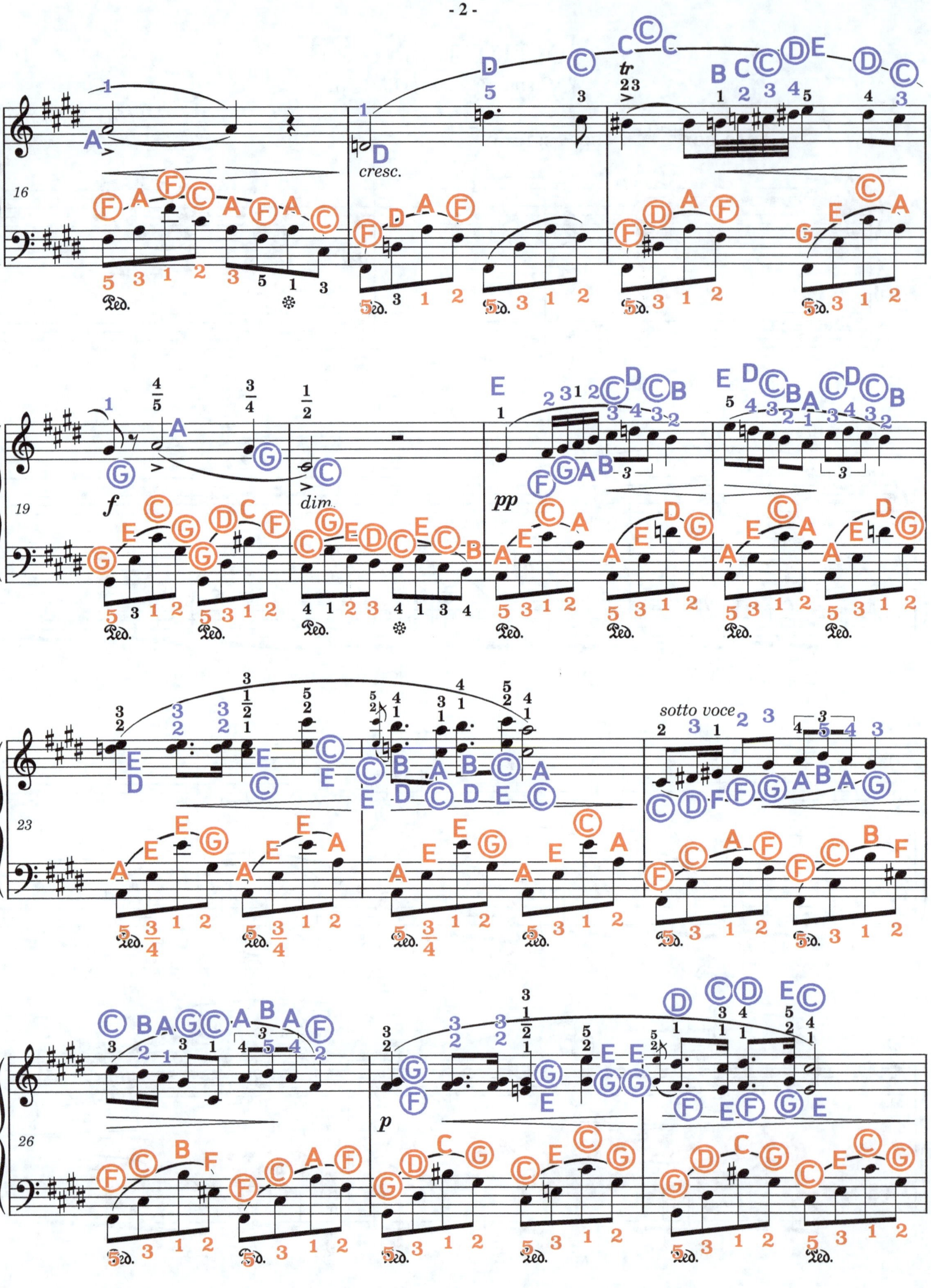
16
cresc.
tr
19
f
dim.
pp
23
sotto voce
26
p

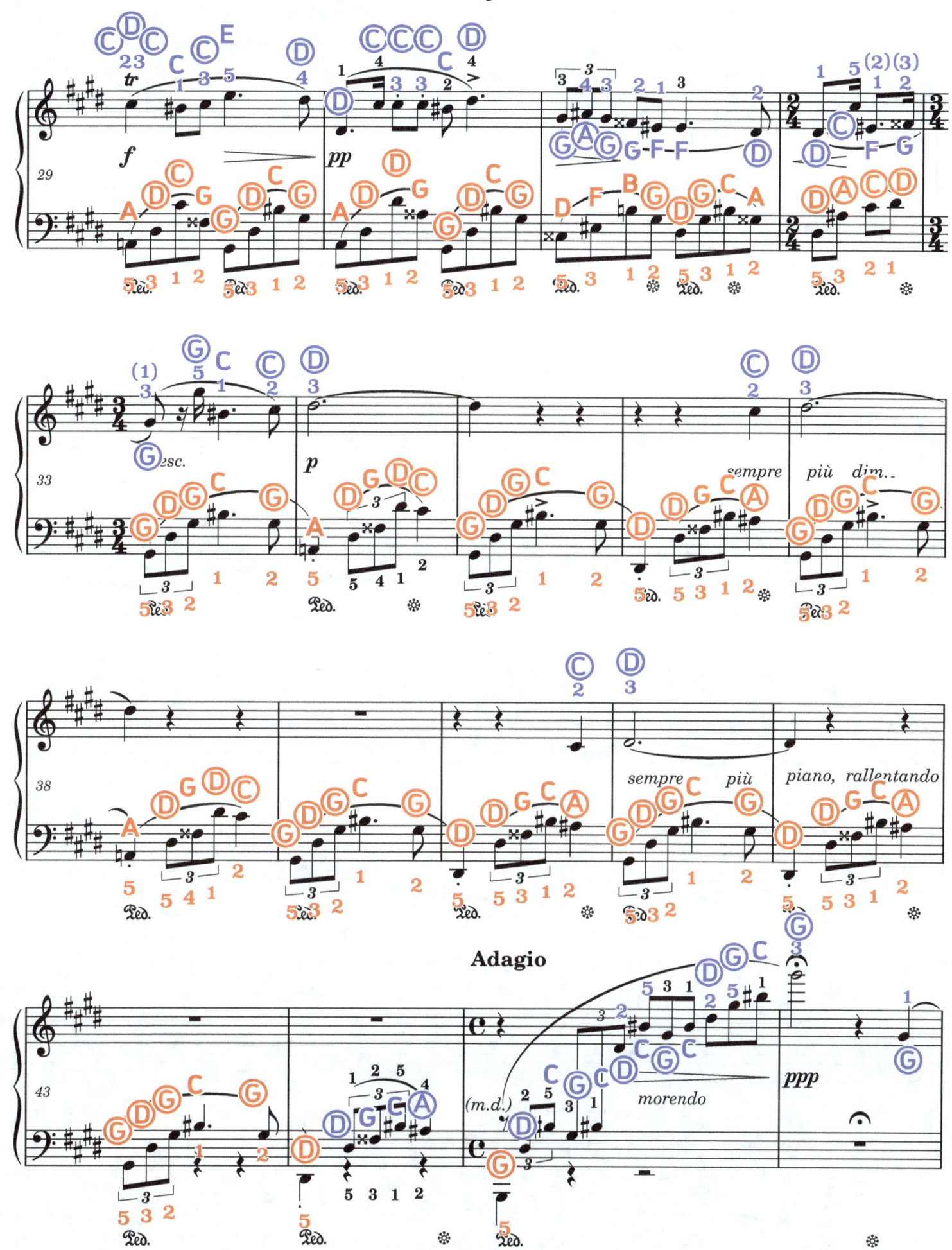

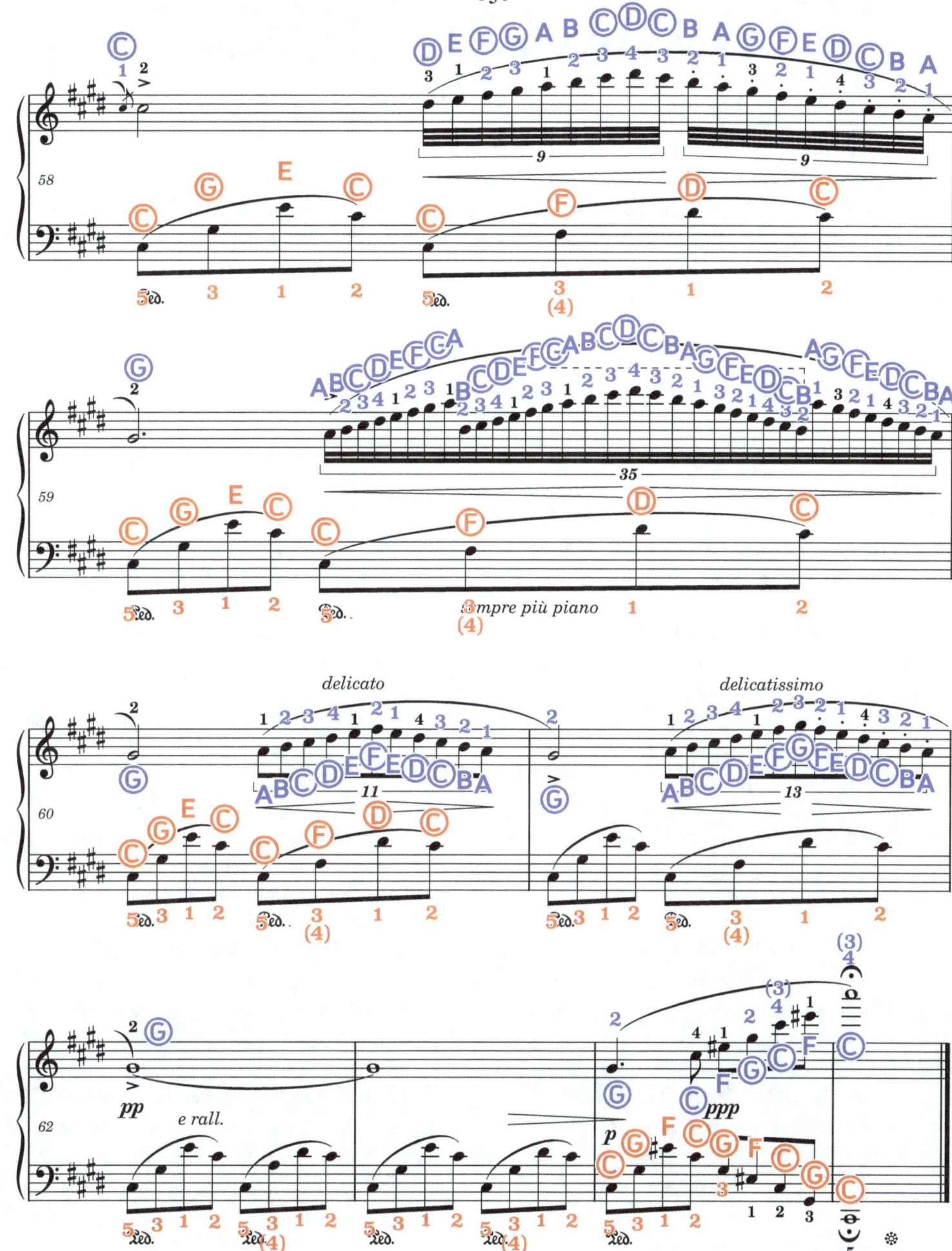

RONDO ALLA TURCA
"Turkish March"

We are completing the collection with Wolfgang Amadeus Mozart's "Turkish March" (Rondo Alla Turca), written about 1783. This is a vibrant and quite classical work for beginning piano students. It is supposed to embody the essence of Turkish music, which was extremely popular in Europe at the time. Improve your technical skills and rhythmic precision with this classical masterpiece.

The following tips will help you to practice and become better.

1. START SLOW
It is very important to play each note correctly, and doing so at a low speed first helps you build the necessary muscle memory. Don't worry about keeping up with the original speed or setting a metronome.

2. FINGER NUMBERING
Pay close attention to the finger numbers, especially in the number version of your sheet music.. Remember that to play smoothly, you need to be able to place and move your hands well.

3. PAY ATTENTION TO THE RHYTHM
A metronome can be very helpful. Set the speed to a low level first, and as you get used to the beats, slowly speed it up.

4. BREAK IT DOWN
Focus on small areas at a time. Mastering a few measures at a time can help you feel more confident and make sure you play correctly.

5. SEPARATE, THEN TOGETHER
Work on each hand separately to focus on its difficulties. As soon as you feel ready, start playing with both hands.

6. READ THE NOTES
Practice reading the original score. If you are unsure, go to the third version and look up the name. This helps you become a better musician, learn more songs in the future, and move past the beginning level.

7. SAY OR SING
Say or sing the note names out loud as you play from the version with the note names. This will help you remember where the sounds are on the piano and the staff.

8. RECORD YOURSELF
Document your practice lessons from time to time so you see what you need to work on and how you're doing by listening back over time.

9. REGULAR PRACTICE
It's important to practice often. Also, having short daily practices is better than long ones less often. Being consistent is key and will bring you the best results.

10. THINK ABOUT FINGER TRANSITIONS
Consider how the fingers change places, especially where the finger numbers are shown. Composers also include those numbers in original scores because your performance will sound better and flow better if you use smooth changes.

Rondo Alla Turca
"Marche Turque"
Sonate K.331 (3° Mvt)

Wolfgang Amadeus Mozart

- 6 -

Rondo Alla Turca
"Marche Turque"
Sonate K.331 (3° Mvt)

Wolfgang Amadeus Mozart

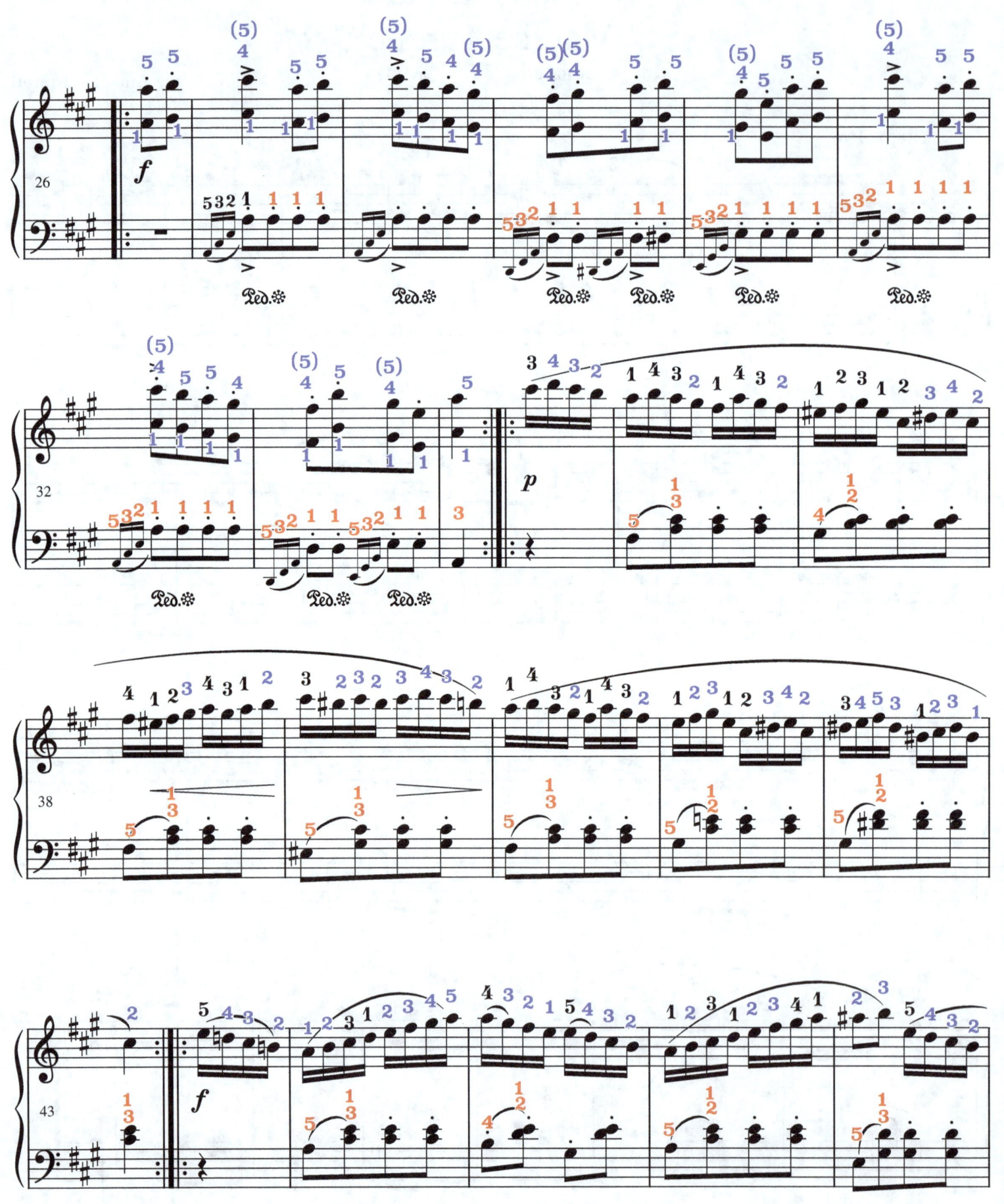

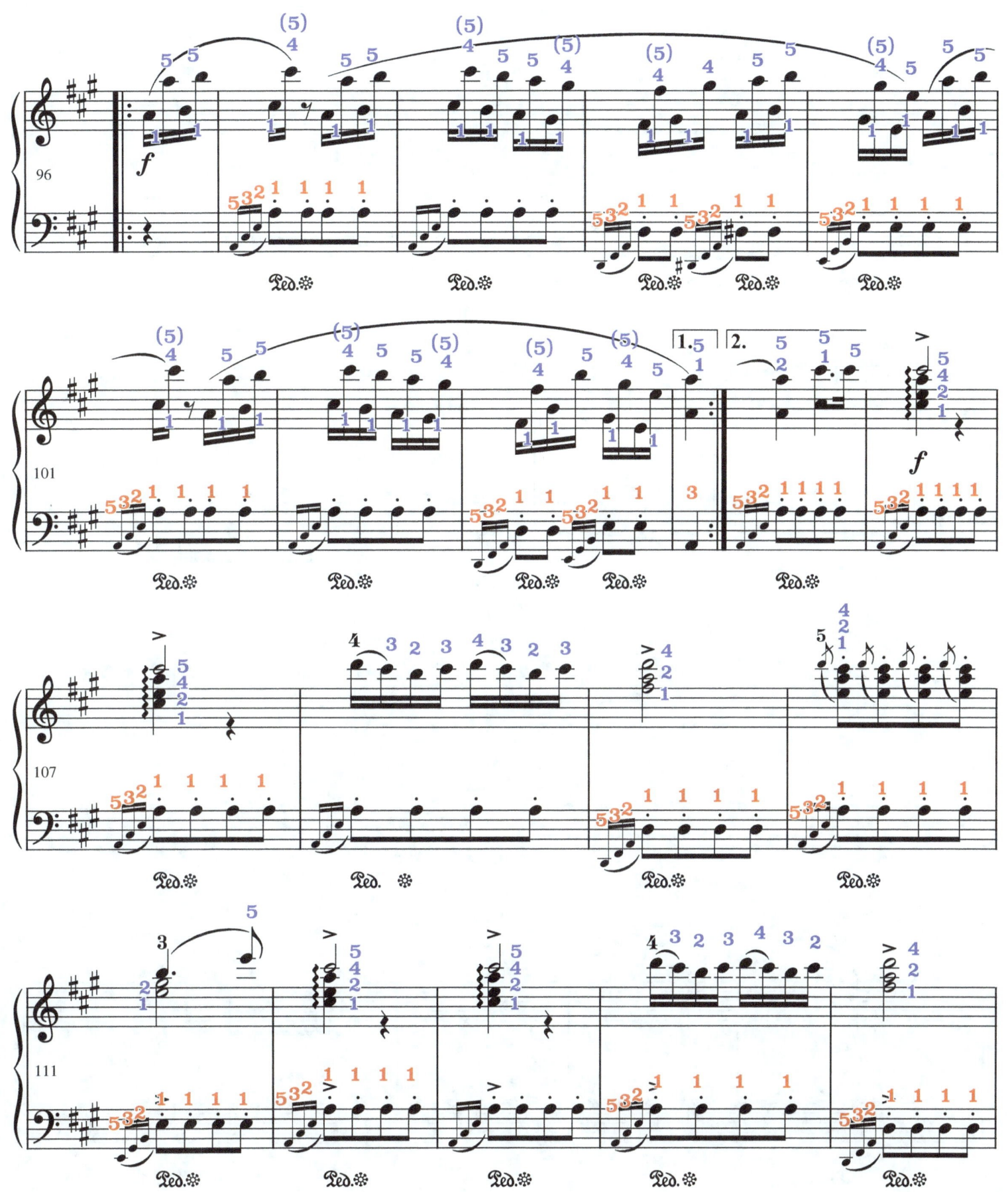

- 5 -

65

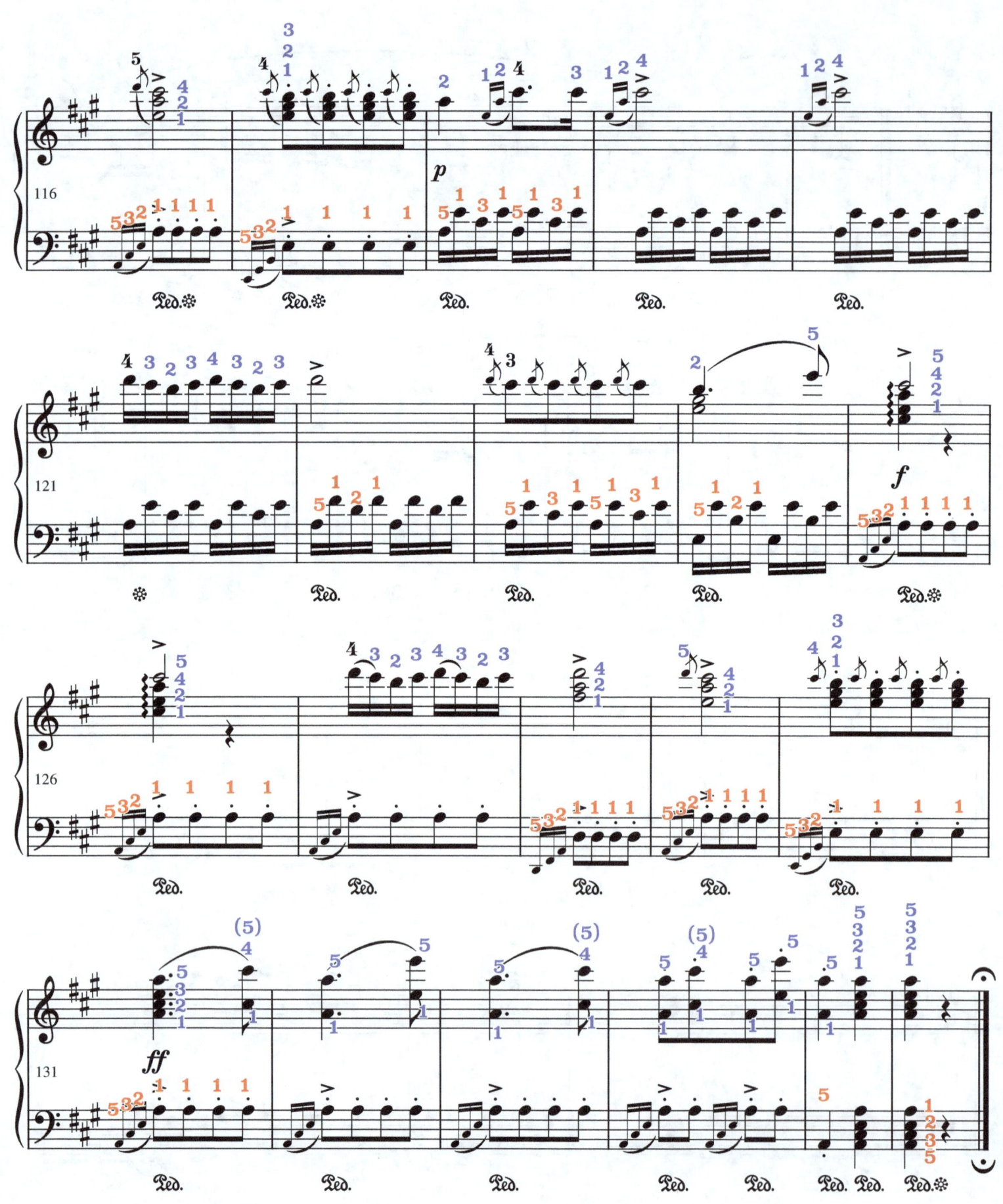

Rondo Alla Turca
"Marche Turque"
Sonate K.331 (3° Mvt)

Wolfgang Amadeus Mozart

67

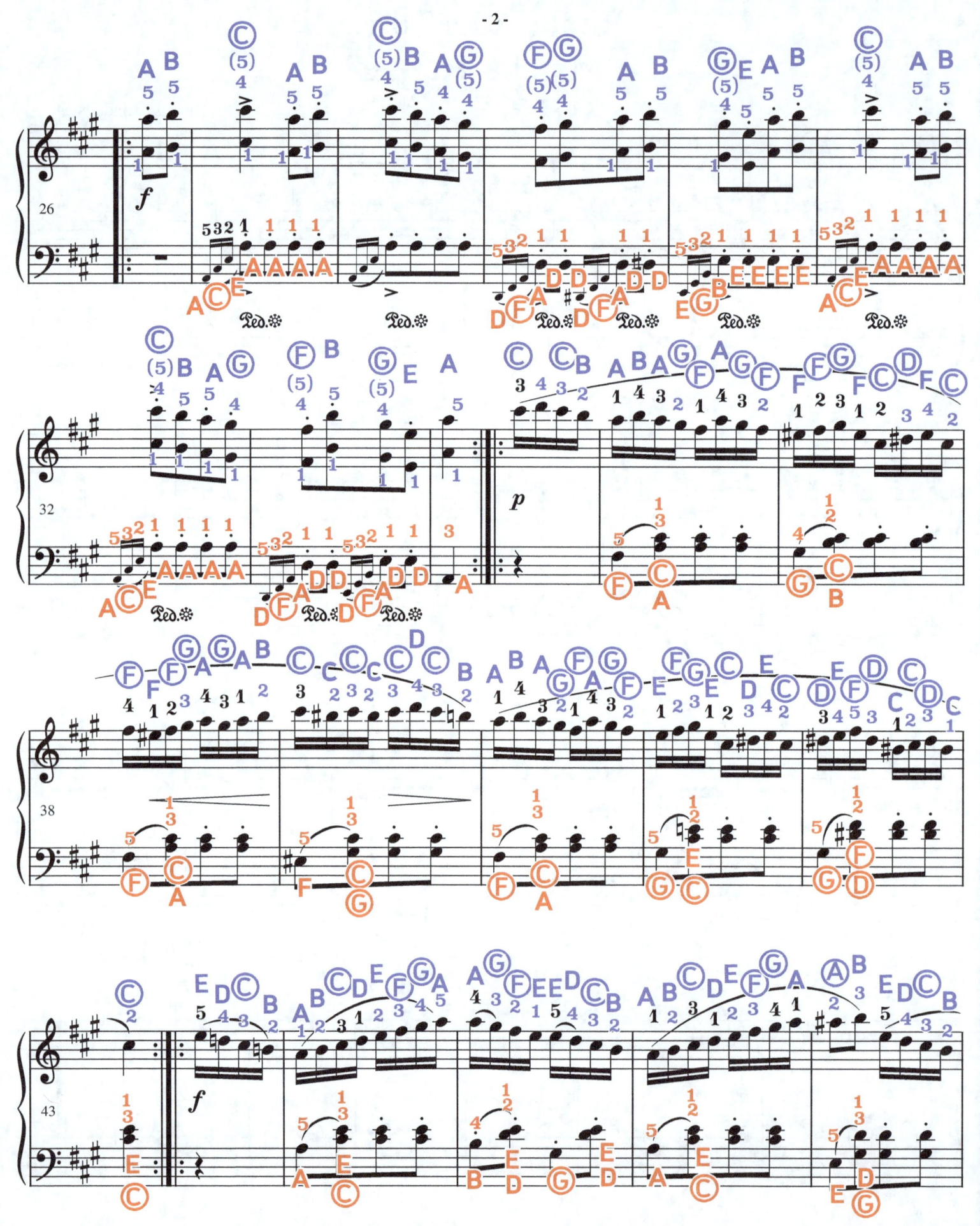

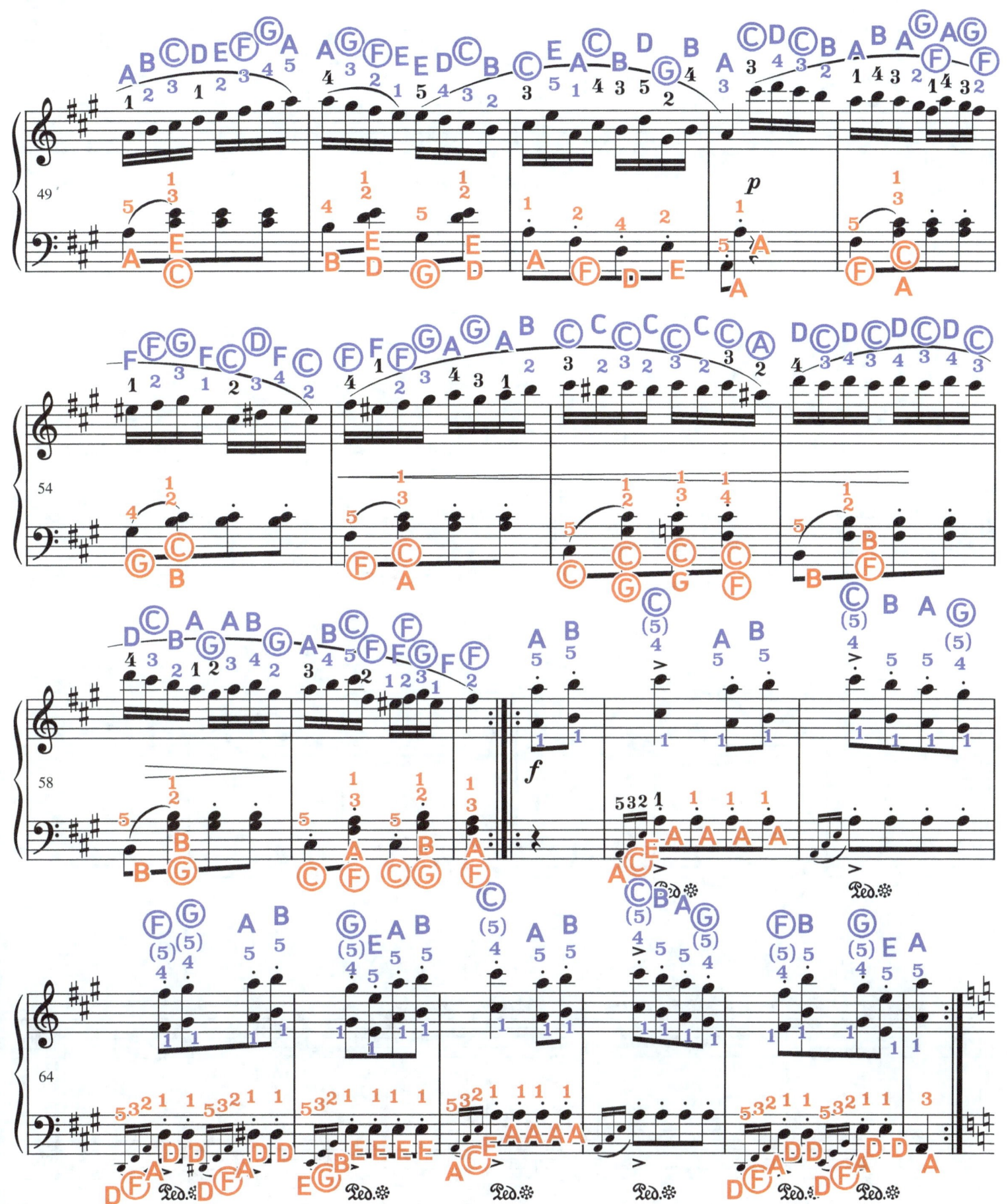

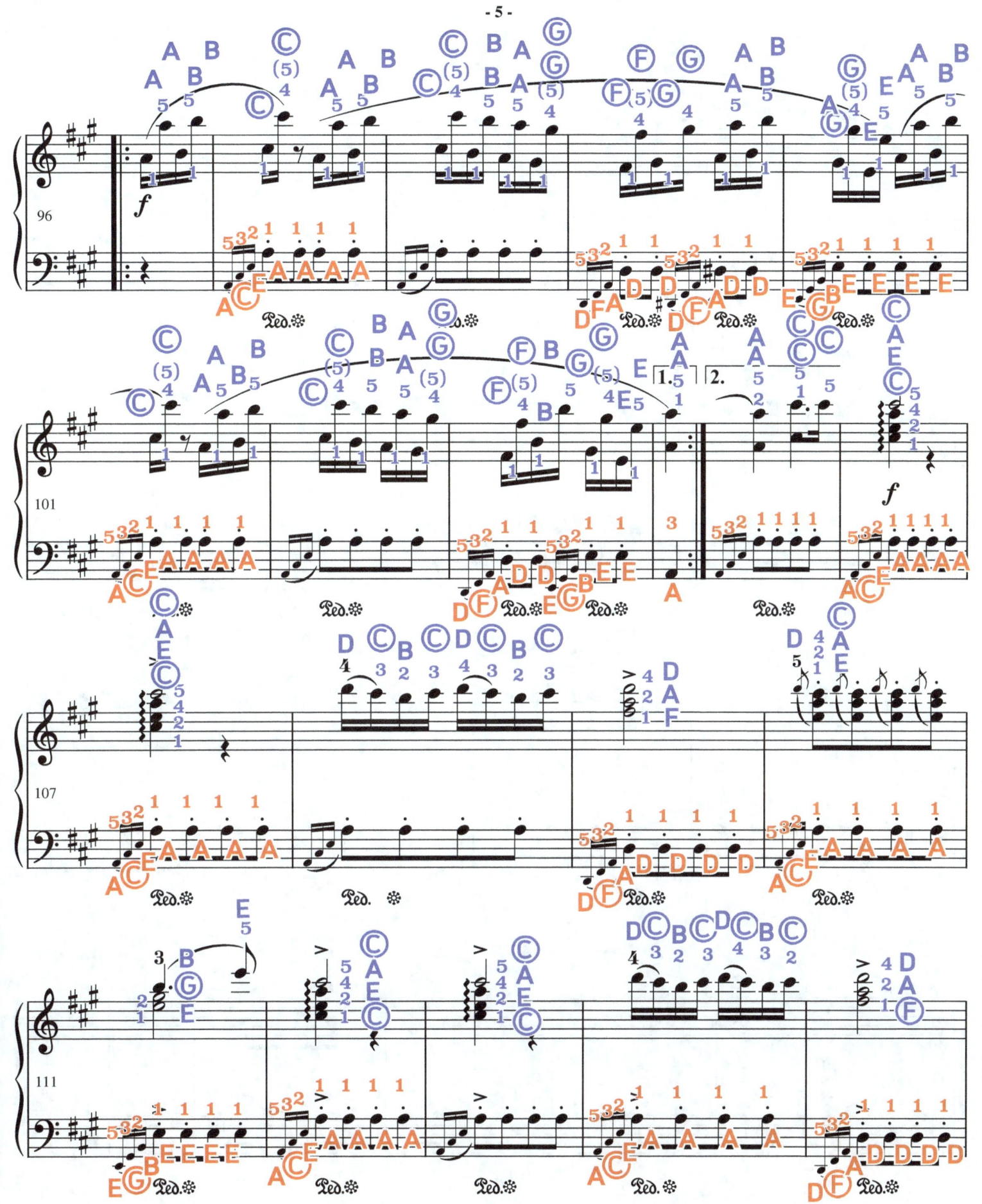

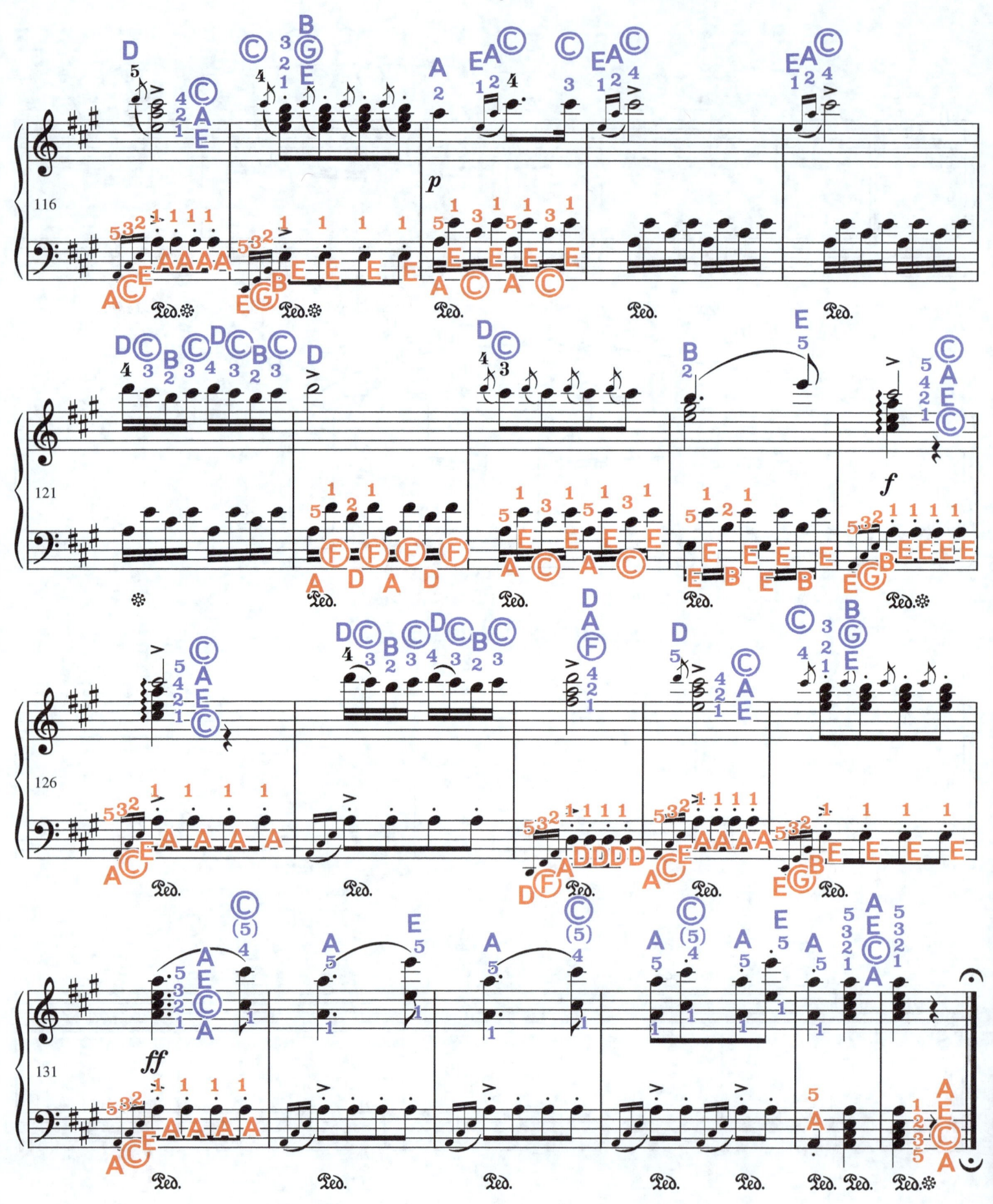

6

- The End -

CONGRATULATIONS!

You've made it to the end of this book.

Just keep in mind, it takes a master to play "easy" music truly beautiful.

I wish you the best of luck on your musical journey.

Cheers.

The Piano Teacher Book Series:

www.HermannPress.com

www.ingramcontent.com/pod-product-compliance
Lightning Source LLC
Chambersburg PA
CBHW081340120626
46546CB00011B/3424

* 9 7 8 1 9 6 4 3 8 3 0 4 0 *